elephant.

---

by siana bangura

elephant.

Elephant: Siana Bangura.
Poetry
Copyright © 2016 by Siana Bangura

Cover design by CVA JAE
Edited by Daniella Blechner
Printed in the United Kingdom
First Published 2016. Haus of Liberated Reading. Siana Bangura.

ISBN: 978-0-9935131-0-7

Dedications

For my mother, my first teacher and my first love.

For Daniel, Sam, and Tawa, my first audience.

For the poet that lives in all of us.

And for the elephant in the room, longing to be confronted.

Contents

Acknowledgements

Thank you to my mother, because of whom all things are possible – my first teacher and role model. We crossed oceans, land, sea, and sky together. Your feet have travelled thousands of miles for me; your endless and unconditional love continues to travel further. No sacrifice was in vain. Thank you for all your support.

Thank you to all those who have encouraged me, and all those who continue to encourage me. Thank you to all who have supported my work, my endeavours and adventures over the years.

Thank you to Daniel Shodipo, Sam Senessie, Tawanda Mhindurwa, Chama 'Kay' Kapumpa and Anthony Olanipekun for reading the countless versions of my manuscript and providing constructive feedback and praise — thank you for always having my back.

Thank you to my editor, Daniella Blechner, who believed in this book from day one. Thank you for your hard work, championing, and mentorship.

Thank you to all the beautiful black women in my life who do the work of love every day, creating safe spaces for us to cry in, heal in, laugh in, organise in, and thrive in. Thank you for uplifting my spirit and filling my heart with love in abundance; it is to you, and all those I have yet to meet, that I dedicate the poems 'Woman/ Ain't I?' and 'Pundersons Gardens' especially.

We exist regardless.

Your black is defiant
Your black is resilient
Your black is powerful
And your black is strong
Too strong to simply wash away
Your black is beautiful
Your black is the beginning
And not the end

siana bangura.

Part i

_____

How it must feel to leave all that you know behind
Forever
Enduring space and time

Nor For Tell Dem We Business

———————————

Nor for tell dem we business
Nor for tell dem
Nor for tell dem

Nor for tell dem we business

Yu see, yu na pickin
Weh no de lisin

Nor for tell dem we business.

A Call To Mother

_____

Although I have never known you
You have always lived in me
My sweet home
Sierra Leone.

GirlhoodWomanhoodMotherhood/ Mum

———————————

(For Mum)

Touch down on foreign land
Leaving all we knew behind
Children of Freetown
Feeling every sound
Tasting everything
She herself was young
Twenty-three
Carrying a baby
Passport green
She came to meet him
How it must feel to leave all that you know behind
Forever
Enduring space and time
Brave and fearful all at once
Adventure some
Necessity more
She is yours and you are hers
And you will need each other more than ever
On British soil.

The Stranger

———————————

A gut feeling you might call it.
I looked at the stoop mum used to sit on after every time you beat her.
Audacious.
You live in the flat that she built as the family home
And replaced us with another.
And the little girl whose hand you hold so tight as you walk down Long Lane
And walk away again,
She does not know that within you is a cold, calculating, evil monster
And that for years, just down the road, she had a couple of sisters and a brother.
You're probably her whole world right now.
You're probably her idol.
And she's probably the apple of your eye.
Your symphony and song.
And you probably love her like a father should.
Until something better comes along.
Wrinkles.
You've aged ten years since we last met.
You look more like your brother than ever.
And there's really nothing special about you.
And as we passed each other, and you held little one's hand so tight
You looked me straight in the face, straight in the eye
And kept walking off like a passerby.
Perhaps you did not recognise me.
Or perhaps, once again, you made your rejection quite clear.
After all it's been at least ten birthdays without you here.
Which is sadder - that's what I ask myself
That you would not recognise your own flesh and blood?
Or that you would walk away again, with no regrets, and no objection.
The ultimate fuck you.
The ultimate rejection.
But I'm no longer small and there are no tears in my eyes.
Our paths crossed on a road well-travelled by.
More than a trip down memory lane.

Your blood runs through my veins.
Daughter.
That little girl looks a lot like me too.
But unlike her, I see straight through you.
You see, I am not a stranger.
I am your flesh and blood.
But I learnt long ago that blood is not always thicker than water.
And that despite Mother Nature, biology, genealogy, and history
I am not your daughter.
And you – the stranger who walks past me once again – you are
A distant memory
A mythological character from a nightmare that was once mine.
You are angry words put together
Curses and wishes that you would just die all put together.
You are a decade of vacancy
Of single-parenthood and poverty
You are the cancer in our society
The man who is not a man but a coward who will be erased by history.
You shunned your duties
Failed your most important job.
And now we don't need you.
But that little girl does.

****

I looked at the stoop mum used to sit on after every time you beat her.
Audacious.
You live in the flat that she built as the family home
And replaced us with another.
But four walls don't make a home
And one plus one doesn't always equate to love.
As you disappear into the light, and towards Borough station
I walk back and ponder on my liberations.
Without you I still reached twenty-two
I went to Cambridge University
And there are people who have heard of me.

There's no room in this void for father now.
No more room in my thoughts for why and how.

I chose silence when you finally stood before me, it's true.
But for all the anger and despondency, I never had a speech ready
No more curses for you.
No more waiting for bad to turn to good,
For evil to repent
For letters, birthday cards, and money to be sent.

Today your myth reached me in reality
The character became flesh and blood once more
The wounds I thought had healed bled once again - they pussed and swelled
They're sore.
But I'll lick them, wipe them
Bandage me up.
I'm a soldier
I'm a fighter
And I won't stop.
A distant memory brought near and brought to life
The maggots in the cave fed once again
The stench is rife.
Some might call it destiny
Some say coincidence
But I'm glad our paths crossed like this
I'm glad I survived the abyss
And blackness is the absence of light
And you have been the ache in my side
Or rather the idea of what you should have been.

But never were.

You see, I am not a stranger.
I am your flesh and blood.
But I learnt long ago that blood is not always thicker than water.
And that despite Mother Nature, biology, genealogy, and history
I am not your fucking daughter.
And you – the stranger who walks past me once again – you are
A distant memory
A mythological character from a nightmare that was once mine

You are angry words put together
Curses and wishes that you would just die all put together
You are a decade of vacancy
Of single-parenthood and poverty
You are the cancer in our society.
A mythological character, like Medusa or Satan, in my head.
But today, today I lay your myth to rest
Lock you away
Get this weight off my chest
Put the tears, torment, rage and rejection in a box
Set them to sail the high seas, ebbs and flows, destroyed by rocks.
Bury you in fire not flood, in flame not tears
Return me anew, pure, and mercurial
And I rise and rise from the darkness, clean from the ashes
And I say
And I say
And I say that
Today, today I lay your myth to rest
Visit this grave for the first and last time
And see that the reflection on the gravestone is not mine.
Leaving you to live and die here thinking you've won
Conveniently forgetting your two daughters and your son.
A mythological character in my head,
And today, today I put your myth to bed.

Nomad Blood

I live on trains and moving things
City dweller beneath the skin
Living off earth and beautiful things
Moving through concrete jungles and finished lands
Taking pictures of faces
Mental notes
I've travelled to places
You'd call the ends of the earth
Writing psalms
Oh the ink, the grime
Putting pen to paper
Repeating scenes
Analogies
Anatomies
Black and white photographs
Taken from a movie
Nomad blood on the streets
Nomad blood in the heat
Prickly skin and open pores
Temples swelling
Nomad blood in the veins
Nomad blood on the shores
Maps for arteries
Settling in one place is not for me
When there is a whole world to see
I live on trains and moving things
Ups and downs in harmony
City dweller above the skin
Feeding off earth and hideous things
I follow maps and list places to go
And catch my breath
Cold nights

Long mornings
Final hours
Final flows
Time is a concoction
No roots and yet I have many
But the nomad in me
Moves through, moves freely
Picks up news and people
Collects stories from ghosts
But is never haunted
I live on trains and moving things
City dweller beneath the skin
Living off earth and beautiful things
Defying space and time
And dreamlike states of being
This nomad blood is mine for the keeping
Through veins pumping
And sustaining me
Until the next journey
Offering thinking time
Ink, grime, ink, grime, ink, grime, ink, grime.

Passport

———————————

Do you know what a black hole looks like?
It's a vast expanse
The type I always prayed to be engulfed by
The type of ocean I wished to jump into
And to sink, not swim
In.
You work hard to assimilate
That's part of the plight of an immigrant
Short of scrubbing your colour off with wire sheets and bleach
You abandon your culture
And language
Close your ears when the Motherland speaks
You're embarrassed by aunties who wear their Sunday bests
Out proudly
Lest we forget that they are African
Like you
Even though you want to forget
And pretend.
You've assimilated quite well
No longer a threat
Almost not an Other.
Few traces left of your migration
History tied to a bonfire
Except for your passport
Apart from your skin
With its pigment and melanin
It is a reminder
When the school bus is held up at border control
All the other kids mumble and stare at you
In that moment you are not like them anymore
You are the child born in Sierra Leone.
The one you've buried deep inside of you

In your crisis of identity
You have stunted all that is good
Now the enclaves of your bones echo
And make a home for shrivelled weeds
As you try to go to sleep
The kids ask you if all Africans wash in mud
Or have to walk miles for water with buckets on their heads
They ask you why you too are not emaciated
They wonder why you don't have an accent
Some make jokes about bananas
A few ask you about tropical storms and sand dunes.
You sink deeper into your seat
Which by now feels like a roasting hell pit.
Your passport is a pass to open doors
As well as the four walls of a prison cell
A Pandora's Box of memories and secrets.
A sign of the things you cannot tell.

Part ii

_____

She finds joy in make believe
For little girls, anything is possible

Haircare

_____

She likes to put mum's yellow kitchen curtains on her head
Before they go in the wash
She pretends each fibre grew from her own head
The long golden locks
She prays for daily
She even uses the dustpan and brush
To brush out and detangle
And she borrows mum's belts to use as giant hairbands.
When the curtains go in the wash
She will stick her head in
Sit in front of the machine and watch it spin and spin and spin.
Fascinated by each cycle
Closer to the arrival of the hair she really wants
The pantry is now a salon and she's getting her usual carin'.
When the curtains are hung out to dry in the sunshine
She will grab her garden chair and sit under them
Waiting patiently for her hair to dry
And get back to its former glory.
Next week mum's going to wash the red bedsheets
And that will be her next hairdo
She finds joy in make believe
For little girls, anything is possible.

Coconut

You speak like a white girl
You're the type that only dates white boys
You listen to white people music
And we know you bleach your skin
Why do you think you're better than us?
Do you think you're smart?
Well bitch, you're just a coconut
Black on the outside
White on the inside.
Hard on the outside
Hollow on the inside.
House slave
Whilst the rest of us pick cotton.

Skin/ Scorched Earth

———————————

You told them that you don't like your skin
You cried because it's too dark
You're trying to be more like honey or caramel
You've accepted that complete snow is too much work

You buy bottles and bottles of the stuff
And you buy perm too
To de-kink and unkink you

You set yourself on fire
Everyday.
Three times a day.

You scrub and scrub
Cocoa is not for you

Hell fires on your head, in your chest, in your bones, and in the marrow
And your once smooth, chocolaty skin is now scorched earth

As you pick off the scales
Wipe off the dried blood
Clean the pus from your harassed scalp
You gently lift the remaining, now thin hairs
In your rituals of abuse

The mirror and your mother are your enemies
And you are the enemy worst of all
Afraid that the sun will undo ten years of hard work
And hundreds of years of climbing up the castes

Being mindful not to swing
You're not a monkey like the rest

And next on your list is your bulbous nose
You want the nostrils thinner
You want the tip sharper

And you want them to slice chunks out of your hips so that you can fit in
And you can wear clothes from Topshop, H&M, and Urban Outfitters
Without fears of small waist, thick thighs, an ass as big as a spaceship
Or any Coca Cola bottle stereotype
Diet, sugar-free or less.

You're searching for respect
Lost your identity long ago on cotton fields and sugar plantations
And you don't want it back

Your skin does not fit with the person within
The jigsaw pieces aren't fitting together
And this is why you tear at your skin
And set yourself alight
And give others the match to do the same
Scorched Earth

And the earth is still burning
And you think that fire settles into snow, finely laid

My dear you are mistaken

Once the fire is cold you'll be left with coal
And you already know this

You refuse the firemen
You refuse the fire blankets
You're addicted to the smoke
And the stench of flesh
The smell of your flesh on fire
On show
Naked for all to see the catastrophe of this one-woman show

And you hate all those with skin like yours
Just in case they remind your white friends

That you too are from a bottomless hole
And that you too are black
And black holes make craters in your moons
And your moons make craters in black holes

Dark sides of the galaxies
And even darker sides of every story

And your goal in life is to marry into white
So that you can at least dilute the night
That you were born with
And born into

So that your children too
Do not feel the need to set themselves alight
And scorch the earth of their caramel skin
Burning everything inside
And everything inside

On some days you conclude that you want to die
Because

Your black is defiant
Your black is resilient
Your black is powerful
And your black is strong
Too strong to simply wash away
Your black is beautiful
Your black is the beginning
And not the end
Your black will rise from its ashes
Day after Day
Time after Time
Night after Night
Love after Hate
Hate after Fear
Fear of the unknown
Black holes that swallow earths.

And you buy ten more bottles
To set yourself straight
To mend your broken
To fix your self-hate
To turn your darkness into light.

I, The Angry Black Woman

————————

Nine times out of ten
When I ask you to describe me
The words loud, sassy, and angry make an appearance
And the curves and the contours
And the ripples of my body
Are othered
Borrowed
Poked and prodded in the same breath
You use to berate me
In my eyes you see red
If you see me at all
And to you I'm made of straw
Packed and thrown into bundles
And stuffed into others
Burnt at the stake on any given day
Caricatured
I am a caricature
And the fingers you click with
And the neck you crack
As you attempt to mimic the way I move my back
Failing to capture my essence
You are mistaken
And when I raise my voice
And when I cry
And I bare my soul to a passerby
You strip me of my humanity
And attempt to block my blessings
Because to you
I am angry
My womb and my hips and my breasts
And both sets of my lips
Are not my own

For you have claimed that I must justify
Why
I am who I am
And whilst other women might fight one battle
I fight at least two
And although I refuse to be a victim
It still burns that you never listen
When I say I am simply expressing
All the stories of my soul
You shut me down
And make this all about you
And tire me out
By saying I've got a bad attitude
And that I am an animal
That cannot be tamed
And you often claim
That all I have to offer is rage
When I whisper
And speak softly
You are taken by surprise
And are fearful when I close my eyes
Don't mind her
She's just angry
Women like her are all cut from the same cloth
They all scream and curse and shout
Scream and fight until their words come out

Hysterical.
She is hysterical.
Angry is her name
Rage is her birthplace
Fury in her DNA
Irate is her melanin
Other women can settle and fit in
But not her.
She is darkness.
She is dark within.

Part iii

———————

I have been known to sleep with wolves
And give them second chances
And chant redeeming spells
Breeding a special kind of sadness

Betrayal

———————————

There's nothing quite like knowing
That there is a person out there in the wild
Who knows your body intimately
And knows all your carefully kept secrets
Even though they don't deserve it
Indeed, there is really nothing like it
And I have been known to sleep with wolves
And give them second chances
And chant redeeming spells
Breeding a special kind of sadness
Birthing a special kind of sorrow
There's nothing quite like the regret you feel when he tells you there's been
Someone else
His mistakes have left you wounded.
No, there is no burn like it
No thunder as loud
No scream as piercing
No bomb as lethal
No knife as sharp
There's nothing quite like knowing
That he's not who you thought he was
And that you were bought and sold
Like cattle
There's nothing quite like knowing
That he's moved away
And he's not thinking about this anymore
All the while you fight it
Whilst it eats you
Chewing on your skin.
Nowadays you constantly remind yourself
That there are more important things
Than that person in the wild who betrayed you.
No, there's really nothing like it.

Hoxton Oxymorons

———————————

I have loved
And I have lost
Walked down these streets
And I can confirm
That all these things are bittersweet.

Balloons

_____

The end is a funny thing
A funny place to start
But I've written about you to death
And chronicled our death
And I'm now chronicling my rebirth.
You're jetting off to Brazil
And I may never see you again
I flirted with the idea of going to your leaving do
And saying goodbye to you
Letting bygones be bygones
And sweeping the dirt under the carpet
Setting the chaos alight
So that it would turn to ashes
And I could cremate you
Better than burying you.
I thought on it and then I thought again
In the quiet of my space
I've said goodbye
And said good luck
And said good riddance
In my heart I've said goodbye again and again
This is the final vindication.
And my pen has now run out of ink
My pen has now run dry
And I won't refill it this time.
I've left you to float with balloons
And kites and hot air balloons
Out of sight
And out of mind.

Matchstick Men And Women

Quiet now
All is quiet now
Struck with a match
Lit the petrol
And watched it blow to smithereens
Silent now
All is silent now
You used the bleach
To burn off his touch
To erase his reach
So that you could finally sleep
Troubled now
You are troubled now
He raised his hands
To reclaim the name
They took from him
To reclaim the name
Man
Fragile now
We are fragile now
Not like the source from which we were born
Not in an image
But ugly
And uglier still
Tired now
You are tired now
Blackened and blued
From his I love you's
And thinking that if this is love
Give me war
Give me blood
But not my own

Give me hatred
Now that? That I can understand
That I can get my head around
Stillness.
All is still now.
You take the match
To burn his hands
Hands that owned you
Against your will
To self-destruct
Erupt
And disrupt
Those hands that made a fool of you
And ripped you to shreds
Left you naked and wet
From salty tears
And forgive me's
Dimly lit rooms
A stone throw from tombs
The tombs you wish to settle in
And be rid of him
Tortured now
You are tortured now
Not made of wood
But you hoped it would
Give you back the heart and soul
That he took
The mind he seized
And left you on your knees
To swallow
To plead
To beg
To live
To crawl
To bleed
And find the matchsticks you've used
The burnt wood that tells the story
Of your open wounds
And his troubled childhood

And your twisted love
And the need
And the hunger
The thirst
To keep going
Existing like this
Because you don't know yourself yet
And he needs it to stay this way
And everyday
You creep towards the edge
And eye the red self-destruction button
Located near the final box of matches
Quiet now
All is quiet now.

Part iv

_____

As you refuse to call me by my name,
You can call me black

Babylon

(For our children)

Black lives do matter
They matter to us
But I'm terrified to bring a black child
Into this modern day Babylon
To be shot
Raped
Battered
Broken
Slaughtered on the streets
And have their killer paid
And endorsed
To walk free
With no remorse
And in arrogance exist
What kind of wicked life is this?

Twenty-three Gunshots

————————————

i

I pulled the gun out from my bag
And stroked it.
Leaned in close and whispered
'I'll learn how to use you yet'

ii

This is for every one of you they said no to
Every one of you they said couldn't do it
You did it
Look at you

iii

You live on your knees
Prostrating for life
Until you decide
Enough is enough

iv

We've settled the score
But nobody won
And I'm still the only one holding a gun

v

Your heart, she beats
She pounds
Disrupting your sleep

But she struggles to keep you alive
Putting work in
Whilst you struggle to breathe
She too hopes god will keep you this time

vi

Take the matchsticks.
Snap them
Or use them
Strike them
Light them
And blow him up

vii

God is dead.
I met a man who made it to Heaven
He said not to bother
It's overrated
Let's make heaven in your backyards and front rooms

viii

You took the bait
Now sit down in silence
This is new to me
But newer to you
I am in charge now

ix

Your soul's on the line
The prayers don't work
You've run out of time
Say your goodbyes

x

Message not sent
Return to sender
Ten times you've tried
But still she's the permanent ache in your side

xi

Eleven dancers on stage
To soothe your rage
Admire the way
They make use of their limbs

xii

They're on the top shelf
The drugs you use to medicate the self

xiii

Unlucky for some
I've still got my gun
Debating whether to use it or not
I am not the only one

xiv

Fourteen more nights
Still dangling in mid-air
Buried alive once already
Praying to be on the next flight with him

xv

Fifteen years old
Breasts have now formed
Wearing makeup to school
Hitch your skirt up a little

Trying to breathe
This is how you find you

xvi

Sweet sixteenth
Friends five years from now you'll no longer see
People you'll hate
And never wish to be
Separated by galaxies
And by now, that's how you prefer it to be

xvii

Seventeen men in the line up
You were scared that none were him
It was dark

And now you can't tell the difference between their faces

xviii

Welcome to adulthood
Relentless and unforgiving
Forgiveness and sinning
They go hand in hand
Let only she without it cast the first stone
You're now legally allowed
To make the mistakes you've already been making

xix

At university grinding
They've made you a promise
You were told after graduation
The world would be yours for the taking

xx

Twenty pounds to your name
Ten in your savings
No idea where the next pound will come from
Living hand to mouth
Worth only the shirt on your back
But still
You have the gun
The deed's not been done
Refusing to run this time

xxi

Iconic age
All things are possible
Landmark birthday
The world is your oyster
Captain today
At the helm of your ship
Travelling further away
Deep into the distance
For better or for worse

xxii

I made it without you
The stranger who left
I spent years at this grave
Drawing pictures and writing poems about this fatherless face
But I've learnt it's your loss
I've learnt to scratch the surface and live after decay

xxiii

They talk about you still
Long after you've gone
They say it was a tragedy
The world did you wrong

You've become a mythology
A tale like Anansi

Twenty -three gunshots
But still I remain
I sit and wonder why windowpane equals pain
Through misty glass
And tired youth
I watched you leave too
But you've lived under my skin for as long as I can remember
It's time to say goodbye – for real this time
I've walked with this gun for a very long time
Twenty-three reasons to pull on the trigger

But since you, I've found one thousand more reasons to not.

Zoos At The Barbican

———————————

Calm down.
It's just art
And with the artist's brush
You earn a license to report, and to explain my story
Exploit
It is now your duty
To educate me, educate us
Educate we
But not once did they ask we
Or anyone like me
How we feel about being reminded
That these people
Put us in cages
Took away our freedom
Even though we were born
Free.
And the righteousness of my indignation is forever called into question
The minute I sign any petition
That calls you out for what you are
The minute I tell you
That you are privileged
You derail the conversation
And make it all about you and your hurt feelings
And how it's 'not all white people'.
That doesn't discount or deny my right to be angry
And tired
Because you will go see me and my flesh at this zoo
And either ogle
Or feel pity
Or congratulate your ancestors for freeing me
Even though they came to rape me
And my Motherland

Fear of all the things you cannot see
But you know are there
And this is why you are terrified

That once again we will rise
So you remind us that we are animals
And you put us in cages
You muzzle us
Strangle us
Use the contraptions of abuse that your great-grandfathers left you
And you devour black bodies
Until there is nothing left
All in the name of art
This transient thing, elusive
Only for the elite
(That is what you were taught)
Only for some.
But the rest of you can take part
Centre stage, in a cage
In this barbaric work of art
That tours the country
And opens wounds and scars
Clouds truths once again
Teaching you and your children
That all we are
Are animals
For you to view, pet, feed, watch
For the next five days
In a zoo
At the Barbican.

You Can Call Me Black

Immigrant. Thief. Alien.
Other type of shit.
Black-British. Convoluted. Hybrid. Substitute identity.
English girl.
What did you say?
Sits uncomfortably on my tongue.
Oyinbo. White girl. Fake.
She is no longer ours. You can keep her.
Sierra Leonean. War. Blood diamonds. Ebola.
When last did you visit?
African. Dirty. Emaciated. Backwards. Pity. Shame.
Child of the rising sun.
Person of colour.
Or just coloured to some.
Brown/ Caramel/ Biscuit/ Oreo/ Coconut/ Milky Way/ Tasty/
Edible type of shit.
Of mixed heritage
But not mixed race, I'm black
Mongrel.
Fuck that.
Londoner. South East.
The only thing that fits.
Global citizen. Child of the universe.
If the cap will fit.
Fucking nigger-bitch. Ratchet.
Twerk for me type of shit.
It all starts to sound the same.
Incomplete.
And as you refuse to use my name
This is all you need to know about me –
Listen very carefully:
B-L-A-C-K

You can stop choking on the sound now
Stop biting down on the word so hard
Don't be afraid to say it.
I'll say it for you.
B-L-A-C-K
You heard me.
As you refuse to call me by my name -
You can call me black.

Capital B Is For Baltimore

———————————

Burn it.
Bomb it.
Break it.
Then build it up again.
You told us this is Babylon
You told us this is warfare.
Loot it.
Tear it to pieces.
Then sew it up again
And this time make sure we are equal.
You are the fire
That cannot be tamed
This is Martin
This is Malcolm
This is Rosa
This is Stokely
This is Coretta
This is Angela
This is Assata
This is Maya
This is Tupac
This is for those who burnt before
So you would not burn again
This is an explosion for those who come after
For all those who have been slain.
This is Trayvon
This is Eric
This is Mike
This is Ezell
This is Tamir
This is Aiyana
This is Walter

This is Rekia
This is for our fallen soldiers
This is for life and death
Obliterate it this time
Then pick up the pieces
Build a bonfire
From which a gargantuan Phoenix
Will rise
And in its claws carry the countless names of those they slaughtered
This is them versus us
This is we have had enough
This is Mark
This is Stephen
This is Jimmy
This is Sean
This is Sheku
This is Kenzo
This is Damilola
This is Brixton
This is Peckham
This is Notting Hill
This is Tottenham
This is for everything that is broken
And the countless people they have broken
Burn it.
Bomb it.
Break it.
Smash it.
Tell them you were there.
Make sure they remember this time.
Tell them you are here.
Build it back up again
But this time let the cement be love
Let the bricks be used only to build up
Not stone to death
This time raise black people up
Tell them enough is enough
Breathe life back into their hearts
Breathe life back into the city.

Sweet Dreams And Beautiful Nightmares

———————————

The psychosis is at 110 per cent
Looking to increase disproportionately
At unfathomable increments
As we keep a very close eye on the news
I remind myself that I have to watch my back
As if life isn't hard enough
Anxiety levels are now at 96.5 per cent, Houston
And I think we have a problem
I can't take it anymore
Father and brother are in the bathroom shaving their beards and all their facial hair
Mother has decided she can't wear her hijab anymore
Not today
Not for a while
And we are all apologetic
Even though it's not our fault
My suicidal thoughts creep back
Where is home now?
I've lost my tongue
French and English do not want me
Je Suis Perdue
And I don't understand
Why the touch of a hand
Makes me jump out of my skin
Friday prayer will consist of blood and terror
Blood coming out of my mouth
And choking my throat
They are all looking at me
Looking at us
I'm scared to utter *Allahu Akbar*
Because I'm not sure how much I believe it anymore
The psychosis is at 129 per cent
And my anxiety is killing me

Keeping a close eye on the news is crushing my sanity
We sit in silence at the dinner table
And then my father cries
And I hear God say
'Not in my name'
Thoughts attack each other in the confines of my skull
Causing headaches and migraines
And my naked head does not know what to do
Strands of hair falling on my face
This situation is always brand new
No matter how many times it happens
My mother has slapped my brother before
She said she saw it in his eyes
He wants to join those men in Syria
Because they understand
But she slapped it right out of him for now
And as I rest my bones
And close my eyes and try to fall asleep
These raging sweet dreams and beautiful nightmares are where I keep my silence
Until I can make sense of it all.
The psychosis is at an all-time high
Drunk on fear and sadness
Trying to stay alive.

Many

———————————

(For Sheku Bayoh, Sandra Bland and countless others)

Don't you get tired of explaining your humanity?
Of counting the dead
Of mourning black bodies?
Don't you get tired of marching
Holding visuals
Coining hashtags
Tired of crying?
I am one who feels things deeply
All up in my feelings
A blessing and a curse
Sensitive to the vibrations
Responsive to every motion.
I am to and fro on most days
Don't you get tired of saying I am human?
I have children that I love
And who love me
There are people who need me
I deserve to live
Don't you get tired of begging for mercy?
Of looking above to find the answers
Of finding peace in church walls
Then staring into the barrel of a gun in those same walls
Don't you get tired of remembering names
Of those that have been killed
Of those that have fallen victim
To the system
Don't you get tired of images that upset the spirit?
Tired of feeling numb
Tired of saying there are people who want me
People who accept me in this body
I know that I get tired of feeling helpless
Of writing poems

Of venting to everyone
I bear witness
To a world of sadness
A tourist in a vacuum
An observer of loss and decay.
Don't you get tired of yelling
I am human?
I have known love too
I know hatred because of you.
Don't you get tired of pleading?
Tired of saying there are mistakes I have yet to make
And lessons I have yet to learn
Don't you get tired of poets
Writing with blood
Performing with weary hearts as they relay the pain of their community
Trying to translate pain into spoken word
Trying to make sense of chaos with every word
Lyricism soothing the ailment a little
Rhythm acting as medicine
Rhymes acting as bandages for wounds
Don't you get tired of demanding one day of happiness?
One day in which to be carefree
Like the dominant members of society
Don't you get tired of temporary recovery?
Of holding your breath
Waiting for the next story
Of another one gone
Another one snatched
Another one torn
Of more damage
And more confusion
Of many voices
Of this anxiety
Wailing over the same things.
In unison declaring
We are many
They are few
Why do they do what they do?

Part v

_____

He is grateful to your mother for making you so magical and whimsical

For making you so powerful

He Is Painfully Pragmatic

———————————

(For Daniel Shodipo)

He doesn't subscribe to mainstream definitions of love
Or mainstream expressions of things called feelings
Or mainstream anything
He won't give you a compliment unless he means it
But he will let you know you are beautiful with his eyes
And he will let you know he loves you
Loves you like no other
Loves you to death when he holds you
But he won't tell you he loves you first
Or stroke your ego
He will buy you a card on your non-Valentine's Day
And buy you a Lauryn Hill CD for your birthday
He will organise the trip of your life
But he won't tell you he misses you
He will think about you
But not let you know that he longs for you
Not let you know that he craves you
He won't touch you first
He plays it safe
And you have to make the stretch to reach him
Do laps around the earth to reach him
But always know he loves you to the moon and back
And he would do laps around the earth to reach you
He is often within his thoughts
But in his silence
He speaks loudly
And speaks with passion
You must know that you complete him
Even though he is pragmatic
Painfully so
And you're the dreamer
Away with the fairies

And up in the clouds
He loves your wonder
And your childlike excitement
And your belief that anything and everything is possible
He is so proud of you
And he has plans to build a life with you
He is a keeper
And you are too
Each night when the lights go out
And the dust settles
He is smiling
And thanking the universe that brought you
He is grateful to your mother for making you so magical and whimsical
For making you so powerful
He falls asleep after you
Deliberately
So as to take in the view
As if standing on a balcony at half past ten in the evening
He paints your face one thousand times in his head
He takes a picture with his eyes
He takes in your smell
He holds you tight
Because he knows that no matter what
No matter how old he gets
No matter how many wars are lost
No matter how many battles are fought between you and the galaxies
Between you and society
He will always love you.
And his embrace will always be your safe space.
The deep brown of his eyes will always be the place that you call home.

Best Men

(For Sam Senessie and Tawanda Mhindurwa)

I have loved and I have lost many
Different
Men
And after sifting through the good, the bad, the beautiful, and the ugly
After learning lessons
And making memories
I have found my two best men
Hearts sincere and good and fair
Brothers in this walk through life
Allies in the noble fight
I have learnt to forgive mankind
For the wrongs and evil doings of one man
From my former life
The universe has given me my two best men
Who hail from the Motherland
African blood pumping through their fibres
Bursting through their veins
Harare and Freetown in their names
I count my blessings every day.

Part vi

Her heart is large
Her love is endless
You see, women are stronger than you think

She

———————————

A simple woman
Who wanted the simple things in life
Satisfied
Happy
Never understanding what we were all chasing
Cooking and cleaning and proud of her home
Proud to serve her husband
And serve the good Lord
Proud of her children
One's a plumber
The other went to uni to study... something or other
And her daughter had a baby recently
She sings to baby quietly
And has taken to grandma duties like a duck takes to water
Humming hymns sweetly
Baking cakes for Pastor Michael
Avoiding the news
It's always bad
Takes cruises with her husband once every three years
Got to watch the pennies too
But there is love and there is love
Moving and existing in abundance
Spending Sundays tending to the flowers in the garden in the afternoon
They are blooming nicely
And my dear
Happiness looks good on you
It always has
And it always will.

Woman/Ain't I?

————————————

(For every black girl who will one day become a black woman)

I am a black woman
And you will hear my cry
Today is the day you will see me
Larger than life
Bigger than I have ever been before
My voice is loud
My eyes are wide
And I am fearful no more
I bit off my shackles and my chains with my bare teeth
And then bathed under the burning Sun
She nurtured me
Glorious affinity
She kissed my black skin and healed my wounds
And the ocean also came to my rescue
Taking pity on me
After watching me drift at sea
Helpless, withered, and lost for too many years
At one point I met God
And I can confirm that God is a black woman
And her skin is rich
Dark with melanin, infused with cocoa
Regal like our joint ancestry
She blew life back into me
Into my inches and my crevices
Turned the dust into specs of power
Ignited the fire in my stomach
Straightened my back
Gave me another chance to walk in the light
With healed wounds and no more scars
And she confirmed that Jesus was not white
And that everything I have been taught is a lie
She told me to exist in honour

With pride
Then armed with a knife, a shovel, a fork, and spirit
She told me to go forth and carve my own space
She said that anger is okay
It is the difference between speech and action
It is my absolute right to speak about my pain
To celebrate my triumphs
To write myself and my sisters back into the history books
Right where we belong next to Madame Yoko, Yaa Asentewaa, Queen
Nefertiti, Cleopatra, Queen Nzingha and Mamma Afrika.
We are the daughters of the yam
Women whose ancestors built the modern world
We are the cradle of the earth.
Strong.
My god, we are strong
We are the people who will always overcome
And just as Sojourner demanded in her truth
When they tried to humiliate her
And question her womanhood
And right to be a woman almighty
We declare fearlessly and unapologetically
Loudly and strongly
We are defiant finally
Ain't I a woman?
Ain't I a woman?
Ain't I a woman?
Ain't I a woman?
Ain't I a woman?
I am a woman.
And we will say it until our mouths are dry
And our gums bleed
Until our chests heave
Until we fall silent because we have chosen to be
She, we, this is HER story
Our story
Triumphantly
We declare that we are women
Black women
Larger than life

Phenomenal in our own right
We are woman.
And I am a woman.

Grandma

———————

Some mothers were born mothers
Selfless and nurturing
Devoted to their children
Then there is Grandma
She did her best to limit how much fruit would come from her loins
But nature had her way anyway
And oh how she has suffered
Lost three of her children at different stages of life
And has become so numb she barely speaks
I piece together stories and imaginings
And create the image of what she once was
And who she used to be
She abandoned her children
Wore red lipstick and pinned up her hair
Choosing pretty over duty
Finding herself for a while
Then losing herself again
While the children had to fend for themselves
Speaking Satan into existence with words as harsh as unrefined metal
In order to cut and bruise Grandad for breaking her heart on a loop
Some mothers are bitter and twisted
They were not taught how to love
And so how could they ever love
Anyone?
How could they begin to love themselves?
Some mothers are selfish
They put themselves first
And their children second or third
Some mothers are lost
Trudging through mazes and tired
Often distraught and distant
Growing further removed from the beat of their hearts

Accepting the fact their children will grow to hate them
Or at least begrudge them
For being awful mothers
Some mothers are guilty
The type of guilt that keeps them up late at night
And plays on their mind
Paralysing them into a stupor of sorry
A web of apologies
Some mothers become my Grandma
The one that never calls to check how you are
The one that never asks after you
The one that never wishes you a happy birthday
The one who has barely spoken to her daughter
Who is thousands of miles away on foreign soil
And could have done with words of encouragement when life got rough
And affirmations of love - woman to woman; mother to daughter
Some mothers are like my mum
Learning how to mother and how to love by watching the opposite being done
And saying 'I will not'
And committing herself to doing her best and sticking it out
Taking pride and finding solace in her children
Some mothers know it's too late
The time has been and gone
But they try anyway
Try to overcome and salvage what is left
Piecing together ashes and dust
And then we have my Grandma -
In her own world
Long since given up
Concluding she's been through enough.
Her heart closed
A brick wall built
Knowing that she knows no other way
Everyone loving her out of duty anyway.

Frontier

───────────

Continent
Citizen
Immigrant
Land mass
She is the most raped woman on the planet
She has been beaten almost to death
For hundreds of years
She has lost more children
Than is reported
Than any other mother
Her orphans are spread across the globe
Being mistreated by evil stepmothers
And molested, fingered, handled by evil stepfathers
She has been slandered
Now she is everybody's favourite playground
All men lie about her
Sometimes her own blood rejects her
Apparently there is no hope for her
She is not a continent
Not a place of 54 states
And an estimated 2,000 languages
Countless numbers of religions
1.1 billion people
She is the unreported world
God chose to favour her
Which then did unfavour her
And undo her
That did curse her
Her womb is toxic
Inferior
Hated
Blasted

One minute they have given up on her
Hopeless they call her
The next she is bright and full of promise
On the rise
They speak about her
For her

Not with her or to her

What can she do for us?
How can we profit off her skin?
Understandably, now, she has a migraine
Sick and tired of these terrorists
She has always been a fighter though
Do you know what she has been through?

Her skin is tough
Her heart is large
Her love is endless
You see, women are stronger than you think.

Part vii

Heavy are the lessons you learn
Outside of the classroom

University

———————————

(For Ayobola Owatemi)

Leaving my mother's nest was not the easiest of things to do
The day before my big move I learnt of the death of my friend
I read the email over and over again
Learning that the face of sorrow could look so much like mine
Weeping over endings as new beginnings forced their way into my suitcases
All I could see were faces
Waving me goodbye
Silence felt so heavy
Tangible weight I was summoned to deadlift
Grief is a funny thing
Confusing and merciful all at once
A stark reminder of your humanity
An awareness of your limited capacity

How hard it was when they left me on my own in my new room
My wings feeling clipped as they stretched out wide
In flight
In the stillness of the night I know I should be grateful
But heavy are the lessons you learn
Outside of the classroom.

Sip

———————————

When you cease to exist for a while
The world will continue
Romeo will keep breaking hearts
The storm that has been brewing outside will keep coming for your bones
And the bailiff will still knock on your neighbour's door and demand each
score
is settled
The pavement will still be full of cracks and discarded gum
And the dishes will still need washing, no matter how many times you skip
breakfast, lunch, and dinner
Your Bible will not have changed any of its words when you return
And your mother will still worry about you
Like she always has
Your sister will grow a little taller and become more like a woman
And that will still scare you
Your brother will be a man
And he will continue to tower over you
The fruits in the bowl will continue to rot until you decide to bin them
Or take a photo of their stillness
Stick a cigarette in an apple
Watch its skin burn a little
In the darkness and in dim light your face will be less round
And your eyes will be more tired
And you might have lost a little bit of your humour
Although you are now a shadow living in shadows
Ignoring calls and texts
Refusing to meet up with other humans
Although you told the love of your life it's over
Because you don't want him to be engulfed too
You are still writing
You are still dreaming of drowning
And the colours are beautiful

Sanguine, turquoise, echoes, blooming
There are days you don't sleep much
And there are days when all you do is sleep
You set your alarm for 5.50 am
And you stare at the wallpaper
Each fold and wave and bump is a choir
When you return to them
Which you will – like you always do
They will ask you the same questions and you will give the same answers
You are okay living you guess.
Sipping from your cup.
Letting it run over.

3.05 AM

———————

Owl eyes
Bat wings
Moon dance
Night things.

Aunty

(For Mafereh Mansaray neé Bangura)

Rest in peace
And rest in light
Rest among other African queens.
They will keep you
Until I can reach you
Safe from this cruel, cruel world.

The First Christmas

This will be the first Christmas
Without him there to cut the turkey
To tell the kids to be grateful for everything they have
This will be the first Christmas without her to pray with
Without him to play with
All their presents are under the tree
And they are still part of our family
We'll set their place at the table
Maybe even a plate too
Carving knife at the ready
But my hymn sheet feels heavy
Her beautiful voice rings softly in my ear

And in this lonely, frightful hour
Whilst others stuff their faces with stuffing
And their hearts bubble and burst with Christmas cheer
I would have already lost my appetite
After the second bite of an empty Christmas lunch

This will be the first Christmas without him
The first without him to hold and smile with
This is the first Christmas that she will receive the cards alone
And beside himself with grief, he won't know what to do in his own home

This will be the first Christmas that you will phone and she won't pick up
And the phone will ring and ring, as if understanding the sadness its rings represent
And the emptiness and void they will always represent

Instead of sleigh bells ringing she will hear gunshots
Like the six that stole her son right from her arms
The six that tore him from her womb all over again

He will know it's Christmas time
But the wine will turn to blood
And every word from their mouths will sound like Ebola
Sound like disease
And that familiar stuffed feeling after too much to eat
Will feel like she is being suffocated
And when they say they can't breathe
She'll see him and hear his last words all over again

I can't breathe
He can't breathe
We can't breathe

And suddenly the mundane will seem extraordinary
And everything will move in slow motion
In time
In line
And out of synch all at the same time

This will be the first Christmas that he won't wake up early or wake up at all
And with Christmas cheer race to open his gifts along with his two sisters and his brother
This is the first Christmas without him, without her, without them

And each person will fall to their knees
And weep
Or maybe hold it together
This being the first Christmas
It will be the hardest
Each Christmas will be a challenge
Things get better with time though
And although that hole
That vacuum
Will never close
This cavernous hole is something you'll learn to deal with
And next Christmas
And the one after that, after that, after that
And after that
And all those after that

You will remember
And they will remember
But you will always remember
The most
The ghosts of those we love never leave us
They sit patiently
They wait until you're ready to carry the burden of loss
They hope the burden will be lighter
And that your shoulders will be stronger

This will be the first of many Christmases to come
There will be many more difficult days for years to come
But you will find a way to cope
You will find a way to love again
You will find a way to overcome this

This will be the first of many firsts
But raise your head
And your palms to the sky
And know that in your heart they are alive

A poor substitute
But you will find a way to raise a glass
To all those we love who have now passed
Raise a glass
And make a toast
A toast to the ones we love the most
A toast to your loved one.

Denim

———————

The route you took to school everyday
Twice a day
To and fro
For seven years looks different now
The chicken shops are gone
And have been replaced with coffee shops
And Italian cafés
The strong foreign accents
That filled the air
Made this place home
The sounds that gave each molecule rhythm
Gave life to atoms
Gave beating heart red colour
Have been ironed out with hot rod
And replaced with Received Pronunciation
And middle class symphonies.

The local pub that stood so proud for over forty years
Is shut.
It has been replaced with fancy apartments
The type of apartments your family could never afford to live in
And gated homes with iron bars and guards
To keep the poor out
To keep folks like you out
The council flats that were the backdrop to the movie of your life
Have been bulldozed down
And the roadmen that gave colour to your growing up
Were wiped out with them.

The air is stale now
Everybody looks the fucking same
They all wear topknots

And have undercuts
They all wear dreadlocks
And wear bindis as fashion statements
They listen to reggae and ska
And enjoy blackness as a theme
Opening up Hip-hop chip shops
And chains like Turtle Bay
Dipping in and out of sacred cultures
Voiding everything of meaning.

They all wear denim
And have migrated from East London to
Elephant, Camberwell, and Peckham
They weren't satisfied with Brixton
Or Notting Hill
Opening up cereal cafés
And lining streets with All Saints to replace the devils.

You see, this is how it works.
People like your parents and grandparents
Built this city
They gave this place soul
Gave their stories
Turned water into wine
Made bread from stone
They walked on water
And fed the five thousand one thousand times and more
Again and again.
They performed miracles
Turned these hellholes
And dungeons of sorry nightmares
into vibrant communities
The type of place people would love to live in
Places to thrive in
Not simply survive in.

Once the building was done
They received their marching orders
Evicted like squatters and mice.

The fruits of the seeds they sowed
Now eaten by others.
Their Harvest stolen countless times
Stripped us of our foundations
Forgetting that we are nothing without them.

We built this city.
With broken backs
And heavy hearts.
Bricks and cement
Hammer and tongue
Toiling with every inch of our lungs.

Now, this is nothing new.
History repeats itself all too often.
In this case, the monsters wear denim just like you.

But where were they when your school organised school buses to pass through
Peckham on route 63?
Making sure the girls made it there and back without being beaten senseless
For no reason
Or cut for cutting their eyes a little
Or Happy Slapped for laughs on Youtube?

Where were you when Surrey Quays was full of abject poverty?
Young working class single mothers in pink tracksuits called CHAVS
By the very people who now want their flats?
Where were you when we took our children to day care, barely children
ourselves, winging it and making a mess?
Teaching them their ABCs over baked beans and chips
Or Jollof Rice, saltfish, and plantain?

Where were you when I was too embarrassed to say that I was raised
On these estates?
Ashamed to invite my friends from Cambridge back to mine
Living two separate lives in two separate worlds, surviving one day at a time?

Where were you when we were four to a bed?
Subletting friends of our immigrant parents

So they'd avoid the last humiliation
Of sleeping on the streets?

Where were you when council workmen called us trouble for reporting things?
Green liquid oozing from the sockets of our hallways
Noisy neighbours
Swear words offending the ears of children.
Big men and big women before we were even done being children.

Where were you when we had to grow up quickly?
Blood and drugs lined the corridors in my part of Rotherhithe
Racists on my landing
Calling us 'You people'
Fearing for my life every time I passed Trisha's door
In case her dog would devour my caramel body.

Where were you when 'youngers' and 'elders' smoked and passed the time
Crowning themselves kings of concrete jungles?
Dukes of all mankind.

Where were you when I sang 'Books from Boxes'?
Retreated to my room to dream of Maximo Park and Metal
Trying desperately to forget the men who threw money at me
The ones who harassed me
And lusted after my fifteen year old body.

Where were you when we raised our families?
Put food on tables against immeasurable odds
Buried friends
And the friends of our friends
Watched through tears as our fathers left?

Where were you when we swam through oceans of blood?
Butterflied through webs of lies and alcohol?
Smoked cigarette butts from the floor
Having underage sex
Doing anything and everything to forget.

Where were you when aunties told us off?
Trying to keep us on the straight and narrow
Looking out for us and our mothers
They worked hard to keep us alive.

Where were you when we built this city?
Built these communities?
Made our bread
Imperfect but a blessing nonetheless?

That's right.
Here we go again.
You were somewhere dreaming
You were somewhere comfortable
On the other side of the River Thames
Internet shopping
Wearing denim
Planning vacations in the sun
And trips to Sudan and Uganda to build schools and hospitals.
You were drinking macchiatos and lattés in Italian coffee shops
Passing the time away.
You were somewhere dreaming
You were somewhere comfortable
You were somewhere safe
Wearing denim
On the other side of the River Thames

Telling yourself that all men were born equal.

Part viii

_____

Do not underestimate the importance of the medicine that is laughter

The healing powers of talking to your sisters

Pundersons Gardens

———————————

(For us)

Where two or more of us gather in her name
We create a congregation.
Do not underestimate the importance of the medicine that is laughter
The healing powers of talking to your sisters
First day of spring
But weeds and scattered leaves are trembling
Darkness is only ever around the corner
Never too far from our peripheral
Vision
But over muffins, coffee, and fruit
We stew over thoughts of injustice
And our insecurities
And what it feels like to live the women in us
The cars and outdoor chatter
No longer matter.
Smiling faces and honest eyes
Accompanied by cornrows, afros and dreads
Fill the four walls.
We've carved out our own space
Right here in Bethnal Green
We've filled our throats and lungs with voices
Our own and those of our ancestors
This urban jungle has now become the greenery of our motherlands
Rich and prosperous
Just like our hips and our wombs
Our parents warn us of juju
But this afternoon we practice black magic
Our chants not in Latin or Yoruba or Xhosa or Krio
Our summoning of the good things
That lay within the hottest parts of the earth's crust
Are done in borrowed languages
That we reclaim as ours all the same.

Words of resistance and resilience
And mantras of sisterhood
Over orange juice and cinnamon
We speak like flesh and blood
Understanding that we are all we've got.
I rest my hands on her knees
She rests her head on the other's shoulders
Coconut oil, Shea butter, perfume, and strength all mixed together.
In this moment, with my sisters, there is no room for darkness
Nobody comes to snatch the light this time
And with these sisters
Concrete realities are, for a snippet and a slither of a clock, subverted into new narratives
Where two or more of us gather in her name
We create a congregation
Somewhere in Bethnal Green black women come together
And love each other.
Doing the work of love in abundance
Doing the work of healing
Defying all that is terrible
And all that is terror-full
Surviving and thriving
Existing regardless.

Twenty-five Secrets To A Happy Life

—————————

Drink plenty of water
Laugh lots and laugh often
Write a list of all the things you are grateful for
Eat what you like
Spend ONE birthday in your own company
Make your family tree
Uplift others
Do not rest on Sundays
Meditate
Read a fantasy novel
Have a meaningful conversation with yourself
Have meaningful conversations with others
Dance in the dark
Dance in the sunshine
Write a poem
Try something new
Say you're sorry (and mean it)
Listen (actively) to children
Watch the sunset
Watch the sunrise
Learn another language
Don't hold grudges
Do learn your lessons
Draw your lover nude (you can be nude too)
Leave your comfort zone

Part ix

———————————

This is what it's like to be an elephant I guess.
To live forever
And to always remember

Elephant

_____

(For Liverpool)

I said I'm proud to be an African
He told me to go back to Africa
I can't be British and African
I have to choose
My waistcoat with Zimbabwean print
My trousers from Sierra Leone
And my bag made with the loving hands of Rwandan women
All offended him
He said white people built the modern world
And this is a white man's world
And I'm just living in it
He said Africans have nothing to be proud of
He said we steal all 'their' jobs
And our children benefit from 'their' education system
And our parents use 'their' taxpayers' money to send back to clans
Cannibals
And tribal men
We spread disease and plagues
The venom seething as he spoke
He said I'm lucky to be here in England
And I'd better remember that
His grandfathers fought in the wars that made Britain 'great'
They created a land of the free
He said black men steal 'their' white women
And dilute the supremacy of an English gene pool
And his ancestors are turning in their graves
He said I'm lucky to be pretty for a black girl
And that I speak well enough
Despite the fact that I speak better than him
Using 'we were' instead of 'we was'
And knowing the difference between 'their', 'there', and 'they're'
Crossing my 't's; dotting my 'i's

Speaking as if The Queen herself raised me
But it was a queen herself that raised me
He said things were better when 'they' had an empire
White people had respect
Now thugs on buses with black skin
And thugs on buses with brown skin run the East End
And the South
And halal meat is funding the terrorists
And all these 'multi-languages' he hears on the bus
Instead of English
Make him feel sick
He said the darker ones are the worst
Breeding children like rats in a gutter
But I was taught the darker the skin the deeper the roots
And the darker the berry the sweeter the juice
He doesn't usually speak to strangers
Doesn't have time for the 'other'
But I seem okay,
I listen
I'm not like the rest of them
And as he smokes his cigarettes
And his wildly orange and yellow rotting teeth peek through his gums
In every puff of smoke and inhalation
I see it written
He is afraid
And he is scared
He should know better
But the system failed him too
Feeding him lies to destroy him
He says he once had a daughter
Half Indian actually,
But her mother and she were burnt in a fire
Anyway that's history
No trace of them left or that part of his life
And he's never married again
Doesn't want a wife.
He says he's not a racist
He's pragmatic
And what did 'ethnic people' every do for him anyway?

I remind him that he is of an ethnicity too
'No', he says, violently
White people are white
And white is good
White is right
Why do you think we align everything bad with blackness, girl?
But it's from darkness we came I say
And to darkness we return
The soil that gives us life is brown
And precious diamonds come from black dirt
And wisdom comes from silence
We're always giving money to Africa, he says
When there are poor people in our own backyards
And single mothers struggling to pay their rent
White families starving
The forgotten majority
He finishes his smoke
Looks me straight in the eye
And says all is lost anyway
His eyes soften
He'll remember me, he says
The one good one of the lot
He says his memory is like an elephant's.
Funny.
I know elephants don't come from this country.
He says he was in the navy long ago
Lost a few toes and two fingers
His skin is like leather
A broken man in front of me
I am loyal, he says
And really my bark is worse than my bite
Larger than life all of a sudden
He hobbles off into the distance
And I could still smell him
Stale smoke
Alcohol and sweat
Bitterness, loss, and sadness
A tornado of contradictions
This is what it's like to be an elephant I guess.

To live forever
And to always remember.

Day One

––––––––––––––

Today is day one of the rest of your life.
All you have to do
Is decide
What you're going to do with it.

Part x

———————————

Thank you

Epilogue

Listen keenly
Stand firmly
Walk with others with eyes wide open
Build generously
Collaborate graciously
Network honestly
Speak with passion
Never hide
Take up space
Thrive in your skin
Learn enthusiastically
Unlearn gratefully
Call out to call in
Breathe defiantly
Seek knowledge voraciously
Read fervently
Heal openly
Stay woke fearlessly

Love blackness unapologetically.

Siana Bangura is a writer, blogger, journalist, poet and spoken word performer hailing from South East London, via Freetown Sierra Leone. She read History at the University of Cambridge, specialising in Empires and gender and she is the editor of Intersectional Black Feminist platform, *No Fly on the WALL.* Her artivism has enabled her to grace stages across the UK and Europe and connect with audiences from a variety of walks of life. Never afraid to address the elephant in the room – the very spirit with which this collection was put together – her work has a special focus on black womanhood, gender and racial politics, as well as family, fatherlessness, identity, Black British girlhood, unemployment, gentrification, disenfranchisement, love, loss, and more.

Her other works include two poetry pamphlets *(Twenty-three Gunshots; A Black British Girlhood)*, a short story *(In Mr. Jalloh's House)*, several essays, and a film on police brutality in the UK following the death of Sheku Bayoh. In May 2015, she became a semi-finalist in the annual Roundhouse poetry slam with her poems *Scorched Earth* and *Elephant.*

Described as 'inspirational', 'magical', and 'captivating' by audiences, Siana's writing and performances aim to touch the hearts and consciences of all who engage with her words, at every step demanding that we look at society with a critical, honest, and 'woke' eye, and do something meaningful with what we discover.

www.sianabangura.com
www.dontgotheresiana.com
www.noflyonthewall.com

elephant.

Haus of Liberated Reading

I

CPSIA information can be obtained at www.ICGtesting.com
Printed in the USA
BVOW06s2056200516

448935BV00022B/196/P